Observing
the Fast
& Celebrating
Naw-Rúz
Around the World

Written and Illustrated by
Melissa Lopez Charepoo

Dedicated with love to

Maxwell and Paul

This book intends to be an artistic representation

of the beauty and diversity of the human race,

rather than a specific and complete representation of the people,

traditional dresses, and languages you may find in different parts of the world.

Printed by CreateSpace

ISBN-13: 978-1542433761

ISBN-10: 1542433762

"O Pen of the Most High! Say:
O people of the world! We have enjoined upon
you fasting during a brief period, and at its close have
designated for you Naw-Rúz as a feast. Thus hath the Day-Star
of Utterance shone forth above the horizon of the Book as decreed
by Him Who is the Lord of the beginning and the end. Let the days
in excess of the months be placed before the month of fasting. We have
ordained that these, amid all nights and days, shall be the manifestations
of the letter Há, and thus they have not been bounded by the limits of the
year and its months. It behoveth the people of Bahá, throughout these days,
to provide good cheer for themselves, their kindred and, beyond them, the
poor and needy, and with joy and exultation to hail and glorify their Lord,
to sing His praise and magnify His Name; and when they end—these days
of giving that precede the season of restraint—let them enter upon
the Fast. Thus hath it been ordained by Him Who is the Lord
of all mankind. The traveller, the ailing, those who are with
child or giving suck, are not bound by the Fast;
they have been exempted by God as a token
of His grace. He, verily, is the Almighty,
the Most Generous. "

Bahá'u'lláh, The Kitáb-i-Aqdas

The days of Ayyám-i-Há just concluded.

Around the world, our hearts are full of joy, good cheer, and exultation.

For those in the age of maturity observing the Bahá'í Fast is next.

It is a time of physical and spiritual restraint,

to abstain from food and drink from sunrise to sunset.

19 days of fasting in the month of 'Alá',

19 days in the last month of the Badí' Calendar.

19 days before it's time to renew.

19 days before it's the new year, Naw-Rúz!

As children, we are exempted from observing the Fast.

We prepare to do so one day, when we reach maturity at 15 years of age,

in obedience to the Law of Bahá'u'lláh,

for the progress of our soul, for the strength of our faith.

19 days of fasting for those who are not exempted.

19 days for healthy women and men.

19 days for those older than 15.

19 days for those younger than 70!

The Fast is both: physical and spiritual.

It increases our love for God.

Fasting and obligatory prayers are like the sun and moon.

They are the two pillars of His Law.

19 days of fasting to purify our hearts.

19 days of spiritual recuperation.

19 days of innumerable benefits.

19 days that elevate our spirits!

At sunrise and sunset,

around the world, we assist family and friends who fast

by lending a helping hand,

reciting beautiful prayers with joy and delight.

19 days of fasting, prayer and meditation.

19 days to remember the poor.

19 days to take an inward look.

19 days that bring bounty and tranquility!

As the Bahá'í year comes to an end, so does the Fast.

The world is filled with a new spirit.

Humanity is grateful to God for this period of reflection.

As the equinox takes place, it's Naw-Rúz day!

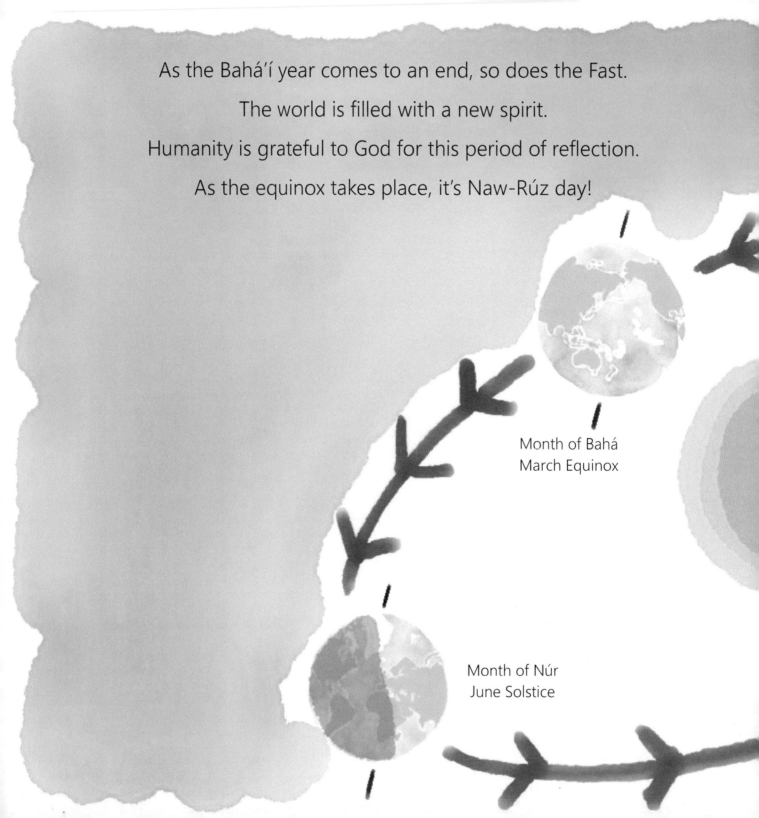

Month of Bahá
March Equinox

Month of Núr
June Solstice

The Fast has come to a close, it's Naw-Rúz.

The equinox has taken place, it's Naw-Rúz.

The first day of the Badí' Calendar, it's Naw-Rúz.

The first day of the month of Bahá, it's Naw-Rúz!

Month of Masá'il
December Solstice

Month of 'Izzat
September Equinox

Честит Ноу-Руз

(Chestit Naw-Rúz)

Bulgarian, Bulgaria

መልካም ናውሩዝ
(Melikami Naw-Rúz)

Amharic, Ethiopia

Happy Naw-Rúz

English, Belize

Tausaga Fou Fiafia

Samoan,
Samoan Islands

ノールーズ おめでとう
(Naw-Rúz Omedetou)

Japanese, Japan

Feliz Naw-Rúz

Portuguese, Brazil

On Earth when the flowers bloom and when the leaves fall,

we are reminded how merciful God is.

For giving humanity a new day, a new year,

to live in unity, love and harmony.

A new day, it's Naw-Rúz.

A day to renew our spirits, it's Naw-Rúz.

The beginning of the Bahá'í year, it's Naw-Rúz.

A feast for our soul, it's Naw-Rúz!

Feliz Naw-Rúz

Spanish, Bolivia

Happy Naw-Rúz

English, Australia

Glad Naw-Rúz

Swedish, Sweden

نوروز مبارك   عيد نوروز مبارك
(Eieed Naw-Rúz Mubarakh)

Arabic, Jordan

Joyeux Naw-Rúz

French, Congo

Felice Naw-Rúz

Italian, Italy

With a festive spirit, children like you and me,
celebrate with our family and friends around the world,
in our communities and with our neighbors too.
We send you loving greetings
from every corner of Earth on Naw-Rúz!

A day to observe, it's Naw-Rúz.

A celebration for all, it's Naw-Rúz.

The month of restraint has come to an end,

with a festival for all.

Let's rejoice, it's Naw-Rúz Day!

For further information about the Bahá'í Faith, please visit:

www.bahai.org

References:

Bahá'u'lláh; The Kitab-i-Aqdas

Bahá'u'lláh; Prayers and Meditations

Various; Bahá'í Prayers: A Selection of Prayers Revealed by Bahá'u'lláh, the Báb, and 'Abdu'l-Bahá

J. E. Esslemont; Bahá'u'lláh and the New Era

Bahá'u'lláh and 'Abdu'l-Bahá; The Importance of the Obligatory Prayer and Fasting.

Heartfelt Thanks to:

My beloved husband Darioush Charepoo for all his support.

Leanna Guillén Mora for editing the book and helping with proofreading
and illustration proofing.

Sophia Wood for sharing with me your knowledge on
Writing, publishing books and helping with proofreading.

Thomas Kavelin, Varya Sanina-Garmroud, Nilmari Donate, and
Rachel Anderson for helping with proofreading.

Elegna Rodríguez and Nilmari Donate for helping with illustration proofing.

To Irina Kashefi, Tayechalem Moges, Hidenori Kubo, Zhena Kavelin, Tulua Smith, Carole Hitti, Shahryar
Varahramyan, Neguin Malkin, Iman Sioushansian, and other contributors for helping with the translation of
"Happy Naw-Rúz" in different languages.

Made in the USA
Las Vegas, NV
09 March 2022

45360937R00026